Struggling but winning

Struggling But Winning

A survival guide for Christians

Peter Jeffery

 EVANGELICAL PRESS

EVANGELICAL PRESS
12 Wooler Street, Darlington, Co. Durham, DL1 1RQ, England

British Library Cataloguing in Publication Data available

ISBN 0 85234 337 X

Printed in Great Britain by Cox & Wyman Ltd, Reading

Contents

		Page
Introduction		7
1.	Problems of redemption — *Israel at the Red Sea*	9
2.	Fearful and questioning — *God's call of Gideon*	17
3.	Fearful and trusting — *Gideon prepares for battle*	25
4.	The consequences of sin — *David flees from Absalom*	33
5.	A poor man and his God — *David recalls the Lord's deliverance*	43
6.	Rest and conflict — *Asa relies on the Lord*	51
7.	Facing the seemingly impossible — *David and Goliath*	57
8.	Asked to do the impossible — *Ezekiel and the dry bones*	63
9.	Inheriting a situation — *Haggai calls the people to work*	69

10. Concern for the church —
    Isaiah's prayer for Zion   75
11. A man in a hurry —
    Nehemiah and the rebuilding of Jerusalem   81
12. Jehovah, great I AM —
    The God who is with us   87
Notes   95

Introduction

Being a child of God in a world that is alien to God has never been an easy proposition. Consequently, there are times for the Christian when life is a struggle. Opposition arises, problems develop, situations seem hopeless, and all these things cause frustration and even despair. But none of this should take us by surprise. Jesus warned us, 'In this world you will have trouble' (John 16:33), but then he went on with the encouragement: 'Take heart! I have overcome the world.'

The problems and difficulties of the Christian life are no grounds for despair because out of the battle comes victory. 'Struggling but winning' sums up the lives of many godly men. The Old Testament characters featured in this book epitomize men and women of God in all generations. Fears, confusion and doubt abound, but so too does victory as they keep their eyes on God and trust him in spite of all the struggles.

1.
Problems of redemption —

Israel at the Red Sea

The story in Exodus 14 of the Israelites at the Red Sea brings before us people who faced experiences that frightened them. But it also shows the amazing resources that were on their side. Difficulties and resources go side by side in this account, as they do in the life of every Christian. Like so many in the Old Testament, this incident illustrates in a pictorial way the experiences of Christians in this gospel age.

Difficulties

The difficulties these people faced were a direct conse-quence of who they were. They were God's people and their problems were those of redemption. If they had not been redeemed they would not have faced these particu-lar problems. The difficulties were the Red Sea in front of them and the Egyptians behind them. They were no phantom problems but very real and serious — so much so that the Israelites were terrified and saw no way out of their predicament.

These people had recently been redeemed. All their lives they had been in slavery with no hope of rescue. But God had loved them and chosen them and exerted divine power to set them free. They had sheltered under the blood of the Passover lamb and had been led in triumph from their bondage. God had done it and they knew it was the only way they could have obtained redemption. Slavery was behind them and they were on their way to the promised land.

What was true of them is also true of all Christians. We are redeemed from the bondage of sin. Our situation was hopeless but God loved us and chose us and, by exerting the divine power of grace, love and mercy, he saved us. The bondage of sin is behind us and heaven is before us. Of all people in this world none is as favoured and privileged as the Christian.

It was because of the blessing of redemption that the Israelites' difficulties arose. If they had not been re-deemed they would never have been in the particular situation that terrified them. We need to appreciate that there are trials peculiar to the Christian and these are the direct result of coming out of the world. Far from being exempt from problems — as is sometimes suggested by the 'Come to Jesus and be happy' type of preaching — the Christian has to face all the difficulties that confront the non-Christian, such as health worries, family problems and financial concerns, plus a host of spiritual problems of which the unbeliever knows nothing. These are problems of redemption, of new life in Christ. They are part of the spiritual battle and Satan's opposition.

Take, for instance, guilt and conviction of sin. No one is saved without a sense of conviction of sin, but this does not end at conversion. For many Christians it is far stronger *after* they are saved than it was before. This is because our spirits are sensitive now to the intrusions of sin, and we feel deeply our failure and grieving of the Holy Spirit. Very often after the excitement of conversion we come down to earth with a bump as we realize that, though we are free from sin's slavery, its influence and temptation still bother us. Sometimes problems give rise to doubts and confusion. We cannot understand why God allows certain things to happen to us. We complain, and bitterness and resentment can soon flow from such complaints. This was the Israelites' attitude as they faced the Red Sea. It was blocking their way to the blessings of the promised land and they could not understand why they had to face this barrier.

Then there was the problem of the Egyptians behind them seeking to bring them back into slavery. This is a vivid picture of Satan and the world pursuing the Christian, and it is real to every believer, whether he or she has been converted only a short time, or for many years. Old desires which you thought were long buried suddenly flood back into your mind. Old feelings of resentment are inexplicably stirred up. The devil does not stop. He cannot rob you of your salvation, but he can disturb your assurance, peace and joy in the Lord.

These and similar problems are real and common, but the greatest difficulty we face as Christians is our own

11

unbelief. This was the trouble with the Israelites: 'They were terrified and cried out to the Lord. They said to Moses, "Was it because there were no graves in Egypt that you brought us to the desert to die? What have you done to us by bringing us out of Egypt? Didn't we say to you in Egypt, 'Leave us alone; let us serve the Egyptians'? It would have been better for us to serve the Egyptians than to die in the desert!"'(Exod. 14:10-12). They were forgetting the power of God which had already been demonstrated on their behalf in redemption. They were acting as if they had no God and everything depended upon themselves. Don't we often do the same? If we let it, fear will breed unbelief. Of course, it can also have the opposite effect and produce faith, as we shall see in the next chapters on Gideon.

The remedy to this fear is expressed by Moses in his reply: 'Do not be afraid. Stand firm and you will see the deliverance the Lord will bring you today. The Egyptians you see today you will never see again. The Lord will fight for you; you need only to be still' (Exod. 14:13-14). We need to remind ourselves of this truth frequently. When in grave difficulties, we need to remember the resources that are available to us as the redeemed children of God.

The providence of God

What a comfort is the doctrine of providence! God had brought them to the Red Sea and he was able to get them over it. Providence is not fatalism; rather it tells us that all things work together for good to those who love God. But sometimes in perplexing circumstances we cannot see how this can be true, any more than the Israelites could as they stood by the Red Sea. We have to face many difficulties that bewilder and frighten us. Providence reminds us that, not only does God have the answer, but he is already dealing with the problem. We must wait on the Lord with patience and trust.

Providence is the unceasing activity of God working in the affairs of his people. He upholds, guides and governs all events and circumstances. It is not the stars, nor chance, nor luck, nor fatalism, but the providence of the God who loves us and has saved us, that governs our lives. Therefore in times of difficulty there can be no greater comfort for the Christian than to be reminded of divine providence.

The power of God

Difficulties depress us because we cannot cope and it seems as if there is no answer to them. We realize the limitations of our strength and ability when we are called upon to deal with serious problems. We are weak and many situations are beyond our capabilities. That may well be true, but it is of no consequence because, as Moses reminds us, 'The Lord will fight for you; you need only to be still.' Is this too simplistic, or is it the truth?

In Exodus 14 we read how God intervened and dealt with both the Red Sea and the Egyptians. Throughout Scripture he does the same thing, for example, with

13

Joshua and the walls of Jericho, or Peter in prison. The same can be seen in church history. When Martin Luther made his famous stand against the abuses and heresies of the Roman Catholic Church, the pope dismissed it all as a monk's squabble. If it was only Luther being awkward the pope would have been right. But God was in it and the result was the mighty Reformation.

We can praise God that this principle is also true in our own lives. Stop for a moment and think of the times that God has met your needs. Maybe it was only in small things, but still it was God who did it. So you can trust him in every situation. The power of God working for his people is an awesome thing. No wonder Paul said, 'If God be for us, who can be against us?'

An intercessor

In their problems it seemed to the Israelites that God was far away and remote, but they had a representative in touch with the Almighty. Whatever their feelings of hopelessness, Moses was still able to commune with God on their behalf. Moses knew the Lord would fight for them because he was continually in touch with God as the people's representative and intercessor.

Every Christian has one who is greater than Moses to represent him or her before God. Jesus ever lives to make intercession for us. We often complicate our problems by forgetting this truth. Jesus loves us and cares about us. He proved that at Calvary, so why are we tempted to think he will let us down now? We spend so much time fretting and worrying, and all the while Jesus is talking to God about us and our difficulties.

In the Christian life difficulties will abound, but so too will divine resources. Do not face the one without remembering the other.

2.
Fearful and questioning —

God's call of Gideon

Gideon was a very ordinary man and perhaps the greatest impression we get from his story, in Judges chapters 6 and 7, is that here was a man with no obvious gifts or natural abilities. Yet he was a man whom God used in a most remarkable way. Many Christians have a tendency to disparage themselves. They protest that they are so lacking in personality or charisma that God could not possibly have any work for them to do. The example of Gideon gives the lie to this protest.

There are times when God uses special men, men of great ability who would be outstanding in any company. Such a man was Paul, whose natural gifts were immense. But it is also true that often God takes a nobody, a little man who would probably never amount to anything in worldly affairs, and through him does remarkable things. Most of the apostles would come into this category, and such a man was Gideon.

His fears

As you read the story of Gideon the most obvious characteristics that emerge are his fear and uncertainty. In Judges 6 there is reference after reference to his fearfulness. The first mention of Gideon is in verse 11, where we find him threshing wheat in a winepress. A winepress is no place to thresh wheat, but he was there because he was afraid of the Midianites. Their raids and thieving impoverished God's people, so Gideon was threshing his wheat secretly to keep it from the enemy.

We see Gideon's fear again in verse 15. When God told this man that he was going to be used to overcome the Midianites, his immediate reaction was: 'But Lord, ... how can I save Israel? My clan is the weakest in Manasseh, and I am the least in my family.' There did not appear to be much leadership potential in this man!

Fear haunted Gideon. In verse 23 God had to calm his fears: 'Peace! Do not be afraid. You are not going to die.' Even the first direct command God gave him was carried out in fear. He was told to destroy the altar to Baal in his father's home. He did so, 'but because he was afraid of his family' he did it at night. Gideon was a fearful man and because of this he was also uncertain and lacking in self-confidence. Consequently he felt it necessary to ask God for a sign to confirm what God had already said very clearly to him. The episode with the fleece was a clear indication of uncertainty, but God graciously consented not just once but twice. Putting out a fleece is not an example of faith, but of uncertainty. Although Gideon

18

said he was doing it so that he would know for sure that God was leading him, when God gave him the sign he requested he was still so unsure that he asked for the test to be repeated the following night. Is it not amazing that God should have continued to have patience with him? Gideon was a weak, fearful, uncertain man, totally lacking in self-confidence. Surely if God could use him, he can use anyone.

There is great encouragement in the story of Gideon for every Christian. We must rid ourselves of the notion that God only uses super-saints. Gideon was a very ordinary man and proof that it is the foolish things of this world that God delights to use. He takes the ordinary, so that all the glory will be his and not man's.

His burden for his people

Surely there must have been some positive qualities in this man as well as the negative? Indeed there were. There was one thing that stood out in Gideon, and in many ways it was the key to why God used him. Gideon was a man with a deep, passionate burden about the state of his own people. God can use any believer, despite his fears and uncertainties, but if this burden is lacking he will not be of much use to God.

When the angel of the Lord appeared to Gideon he greeted him with the rather formal words: 'The Lord is with you, mighty warrior.' Gideon was anything but a mighty warrior, but he was a spiritual man and there was no formality about his answer: 'If the Lord is with us, why has all this happened to us? Where are all his wonders that our fathers told us about?' His answer exposes the burden of his heart. He asks, 'If the Lord is with us, why are we so weak and helpless? Where are the evidences of his presence?' It is easy for a Christian to accept blandly the statement that God is with him, without any concern to know the divine presence experimentally. How often we claim the promise, 'Where two or three come together in my name, there am I with them' (Matt. 18:20), yet seem unconcerned to know the manifest presence of the Lord. Just to say, 'The Lord is with us,' in a vague, theoretical way is not enough. We need to *know* that God is with us. In spite of all his faults and weaknesses, Gideon was not prepared to accept the theoretical statement: 'The Lord is with you.' He wanted to experience, to see, the evidence of God's presence. This is not only reasonable, but is an essential mark of a spiritual man.

The weak spiritual condition of God's people deeply concerned Gideon and he wanted to see demonstrations of the power of God like those that had been experienced in the past. He had heard about such things but he could not be satisfied merely with hearing, he wanted to experience them himself. That was his thinking, but what right did he have to expect to see a repeat of God's wonders? He had the authority of God's assurance that 'The Lord is with you.' In biblical terms this means the demonstration of the presence and power of God. If what the angel said was true, Gideon wanted to see the evidence of God's presence.

A necessary question

Gideon's question, 'If the Lord is with us, why has all this happened to us?' is one to challenge much of modern evangelical complacency. Where today is the sense of the presence of the Lord? Where is the mighty hand of God that we read of in the history books? Gideon's question was right, legitimate and necessary, and it still is. We must not accept the great promises and statements of the Bible in an empty, theoretical way. If the Lord is with us, why is Christianity so weak today? If the Lord is with us, why are we not seeing great demonstrations of his power, as in the days of Whitefield and Wesley?

In a measure, Gideon knew the answer to these questions. He went on: 'The Lord has abandoned us and put us into the hand of Midian' (Judg. 6:13). There is no doubt that this is the only explanation for the sorry predicament that he and his fellow Israelites were in. But why had the Lord abandoned them? The answer is given twice in Judges 6. Firstly, 'The Israelites did evil in the eyes of the Lord' (v. 1), and secondly, 'You have not listened to me' (v. 10). In other words, their problems were a consequence of sin.

God's answer

We need to remember that in the story of Gideon we do not see God dealing with the world, but with his own redeemed people. They were the covenant people of God,

21

but they had sinned and refused to listen to the Lord, so he had allowed the Midianites to dominate them. Gideon recognized the results, but did he acknowledge the reason? Did he know why God had abandoned them? The Israelites certainly did not. In verse 6 we find them in acute distress crying to God for help, but there is no sense of repentance. Their cry was merely a reaction to physical discomfort.

Because there was no repentance, the Lord's first response to their cry was not to send them Gideon as a deliverer, but to send a nameless prophet (Judg. 6:7-10) to tell them why they were in their present trouble. God insists that his people recognize the problem. They thought the problem was the Midianites and God showed them that the real cause of their troubles was their own sin. The Midianites were only tools in the hand of God to deal with his people.

Many Christians today see the terrible state of the church. They see that biblical Christianity seems so helpless and weak against the forces of evil all around. They see the spiritual and moral decline in the nation and cry to God for revival. As the Israelites wanted God to deal with Midian, so Christians want God to deal with the world. But the world is not the problem; the church is the problem. A true prayer for revival can only ever be the product of a deep conviction of sin. The prayer for revival is always a prayer of repentance. It is to acknowledge that my spiritual life, and the life of the church, is not what it should be. Revival means to bring back the life that was once vibrant and effective; it means to rekindle the dying flame. The world does not need reviving; the world needs regenerating. It is the church that needs reviving, and a revived church abounding with the life and power of the Holy Spirit is God's answer to a decadent and godless world.

Unless we can see and appreciate this, we shall be like the Israelites before Midian, and go on trying out our little schemes to seek to frustrate the forces of evil. Running away from the problems (Judg. 6:2), or threshing wheat in a winepress to avoid contact with the enemy (Judg. 6:11), is no substitute for repentance. Until we see the real problem, we shall always be playing around with our own schemes and ideas, and they will be as pathetic and useless as were the Israelites' schemes. The answer is the Lord. And thus God's first demand is that we see our sin and repent, so that we can experience again the power of God at work in our lives and in our land.

Hope

The story of Gideon, fearful and questioning, should give us great hope. The Israelites deserved nothing, but God heard their cry and intervened on their behalf. The reason for this hope is in a phrase that occurs many times in the Old Testament. We read it first in Genesis 9:15: 'I will remember my covenant between me and you.' It means that God is faithful to his covenant promises even though we, his people, forget them. The Christian church is the covenant people of God. It is a covenant sealed in the blood of Jesus and God will always remember it. This is our hope. God has loved us and redeemed us but we still sin and deserve nothing, yet because of the covenant we can cry, 'Lord, for the sake of Jesus, for the glory of his name, vindicate your honour in our land.'

Gideon was right to ask, 'Where are all the wonders that our fathers told us about?' We are right to long for the blessings on our land that we read happened in previous centuries. We may be fearful, uncertain and lacking in confidence, but these are not the things that really matter. What God is looking for is that we have hearts concerned about the spiritual state of our nation and the lack of power of our churches. Such hearts God can and will bless. Such Christians God can and will use.

3.
Fearful and trusting —

Gideon prepares for battle

In Judges 6 we see God preparing Gideon for service, and in chapter 7 we see God using Gideon. Gideon's basic fearfulness never changed, but it did not stop him trusting the Lord.

Midian had an army of 135,000 men (Judg. 8:10), and when Gideon had at last accepted the fact that God was going to use him, he set about raising an army of Israelites to oppose this vast army. It was the obvious thing to do, but the most Gideon could amass was 32,000 soldiers. So immediately this timid man was confronted with the fact that his best was not going to be good enough. He was still outnumbered by over four to one. Gideon was discovering what most Christians have discovered in their service for God. But this fact is not to discourage us, because in the spiritual battles we have to face we are never left to our own resources.

The great declaration of Scripture is that the battle is the Lord's. Whether it is a battle with self and our own weakness, or a battle on a different field with Satan's armies, this truth is still to be claimed and acted upon. The Christian has resources far above his natural strength and abilities. If this were not so, we would spend most of our time in utter and complete despair.

Faith tested

God taught this great truth to Gideon in a most unusual way. The main lesson of Judges 7 is not how God dealt with the Midianites, because in a sense they are irrelevant, but how God dealt with his people.

Gideon wanted to see the wonders and power of God, but before this his faith was severely tested by the Lord. Gideon had to learn the lesson that God's ways are not our ways. He had to be faced with the reality that 'Though we live in the world, we do not wage war as the world does. The weapons we fight with are not the weapons of the world. On the contrary, they have divine power to demolish strongholds' (2 Cor. 10:3-4). As the Lord taught his servant this truth and as he worked out the principle of God-centred activity in the life of an ordinary man, the Lord applied the truth in a most remarkable way. Gideon was told that his problem was not that his army was too small, but that it was too large!

This was the last thing Gideon expected to hear from God. He had probably spent sleepless nights worrying where he was going to find another 100,000 soldiers in order to achieve some sort of numerical balance with the enemy. Yet he was told to do something which resulted in 22,000 of his men leaving. And even that was not the end, for eventually God whittled Gideon's army down to 300 men. Everything about God's dealing with this man was stretching his faith to the limit. It was all contrary to human thinking and strategy, but it was not without purpose or reason. The reason was that 'You have too many men for me to deliver Midian into their hands. In order that Israel may not boast against me that her own strength has saved her...' God was making it abundantly clear that the coming victory was from him and him alone. He was removing any possibility of the Israelites boasting in the achievement of their small army. When 300 defeated 135,000 there could be only one explanation: the Lord had done this.

A basic principle

How do we react to the story of God's dealing with Gideon? Do we see it as a quaint Old Testament story, or do we see it as a basic biblical principle? It is a failure to take such Old Testament events seriously, and to apply them to our own personal Christian lives and to the corporate life of our churches, that has led to much of the stagnation and defeatism of present-day Christianity.

The story demonstrates a truth running right through the Bible, namely that the world has its methods, and God has his way of doing things. It is because we forget this that the church has allowed the most bizarre methods to be introduced into its life, and particularly into its evangelism. There is a desperate need today for the church to be relevant in its message to the world and to speak in language and concepts that modern man can understand. We are not living in the nineteenth century and to preach today as if we were is to deny the relevance of the gospel to this generation of sinners. But this is no excuse for methods of evangelism that are taken straight out of the world. The Acts of the Apostles is still the best textbook on evangelism and there is no substitute for the power of the Holy Spirit. To forget this is to go down a very slippery path. God does not need multi-media presentations or dubious entertainment and sports stars to make his gospel successful. Neither is he confined to antiquarian language and style. We have had our fill of both these extremes and we still find ourselves asking Gideon's question: 'Where are the wonders that our fathers told us about?'

If God is to do such works in our day it will be so that Judges 7:2 is seen to be true. It will be in such a way that it is obvious that God is working, not man. The results must be clearly seen to be the consequences not of man's cleverness and schemes, but of the power of God. The Lord showed Gideon that what was needed was not plans, schemes and gimmicks, but the power and presence of God. We need to learn that lesson today.

Two kinds of fear

The dominant emotion that emerges in Judges 6 and 7 is that of fear. We have seen that Gideon himself was a very fearful man. And the test that reduced the army by 22,000 men was that 'Anyone who trembles with fear may turn back and leave' (Judg. 7:3). Gideon never lost that fear and God knew this (Judg. 7:10), but still he was used by the Lord. This was because there are two kinds of fear. There is the fear that paralyses, and the fear that casts itself on the Lord. When Gideon was commanded to pull down the altar of Baal in his father's house he was afraid, so he did it at night — but he did it. The 22,000 would have been afraid and done nothing because their fear would have rendered them incapable. Gideon's fear led him to depend upon the strength of God.

Here is a perfect example that fear need be no hindrance to service. Many of us are frequently riddled with fears — fear to witness, fear to pray in a prayer meeting. Most Christians have these or similar fears. What do we do with them? Do not let them dominate your Christian life. Recognize them and face up to them, and then do what God wants you to do in his strength. Remember Gideon, and recognize that fear can be translated into action. We are not told in Scripture just to be strong, but to be strong in the Lord and the power of his might. Very few are strong in their own strength and, strangely, often our own strength can be more of a hindrance than a help in Christian work. Self-confidence is a real hindrance to effective, God-honouring Christian service. There are fears and fears. If your fear is paralysing you, think of Gideon. One of our greatest strengths can be to know our own inabilities, and then to trust the Lord for his strength to work through us.

God understands our fears

There is another encouragement in this story for those
who are fearful: God understands our fears. We see this
in Judges 7:10-15. Not only does God understand our
fears, but he ministers to us in them. Because Gideon was
still afraid, God gave him the remarkable encouragement
found in these verses. It must have taken a great deal of
faith for Gideon to obey God and go with only his servant
into the Midianite camp. The sight that greeted his eyes
would have terrified him. We are told that the enemy 'had
settled in the valley, thick as locusts'. And to emphasize
this further the Scripture adds, 'Their camels could no
more be counted than the sand on the sea shore' (Judg.
7:12). When Gideon saw this and remembered that his
own army now consisted of only 300 men, he must have
been totally demoralized.

Then Gideon had a bit of luck! He 'arrived just as a
man was telling his friend his dream'. Five minutes later
and he would have missed this, but how fortunate that he
arrived just at the right time! Of course, this was no luck
but the goodness of God to his servant. It was all planned
by God to encourage this fearful saint and it worked
because Gideon returned to his camp brimming with the
confidence that the Lord was going to give him a great
victory.

God knows that very few, if any, of us are going to be
super-saints with no fears or doubts. He does not expect
us to be like that, but he does expect us to love him in spite
of our doubts. He expects us to obey him and trust him in

spite of our fears. When we do, he graciously ministers to us in our weakness, just as he did with Gideon. We should not think that this man's experience was unique and that we could never know anything similar. On the contrary, it can also be our experience and almost certainly has been at some time in our Christian life. Have there not been times when we were afraid, yet the Lord drew near in some simple way to encourage us? As a result we trusted and obeyed in spite of the fear and were greatly blessed because of it. God works like that because he loves us and wants to use us.

The battle

The story of the battle is well known and thrilling and leads us to gasp in wonder at the might and power of our God. Is anything impossible for God? And because we are the people of God it means that there is no situation that can confront us as Christians that is hopeless. If the Lord is with us there is no such thing as hopelessness. The God of Gideon, of Moses, of David is our God. The God who performed wonders in the days of past revivals is still the same God and can still turn this world upside down.

God stretched Gideon's faith almost to breaking-point and he may do the same with us, but he always has a purpose. We need to learn the lesson of Gideon that very ordinary folk can become invincible when they lean exclusively upon the strength of God.

4.
The consequences of sin —

David flees from Absalom

Psalm 3 comes out of what was one of the saddest experiences in David's life. He had known many trials and disappointments but none like this. His son Absalom was rebelling against him and seeking the throne for himself. David had known much opposition in his life, particularly from King Saul, but this was different — this was his own son. We learn of the incident in 2 Samuel 15, and there we read in verse 30 that this man of God wept bitterly as he contemplated this most severe of all opposition. If this were not enough to cope with, David was told that Ahithophel had joined forces with Absalom. This man had been one of his closest friends and had served well as David's chief adviser. The king's high regard for Ahithophel is shown us in 2 Samuel 16:23, where we are told that 'The advice Ahithopel gave was like that of one who enquires of God.' This opposition was a bitter pill for David to swallow. He laments,

Even my close friend, whom I trusted,
   he who shared my bread,
   has lifted up his heel against me

(Ps. 41:9).

Troubles rarely come singly. Often they crowd upon one another and seem to compete to pull us down. Son and best friend act against this man of God. It is the experience of most of us that what we can take bravely from strangers becomes a bitter blow when inflicted by loved ones. David laments:

If an enemy were insulting me,
   I could endure it;
if a foe were raising himself against me,
   I could hide from him.
But it is you, a man like myself,
   my companion, my close friend,
with whom I once enjoyed sweet fellowship
   as we walked with the throng at the house of God

(Ps. 55:12-14).

Spurgeon comments on these verses: 'Reproaches from those who have been intimate with us, and trusted by us, cut us to the quick; and they are usually so well acquainted with our peculiar weaknesses that they know how to touch us where we are most sensitive, and to speak so as to do us most damage. The slanders of an avowed antagonist are seldom so mean and dastardly as those of a traitor, and the absence of the elements of ingratitude and treachery renders them less hard to bear.'[1]

David's reaction

How are we to react as Christians in a situation like this? That will depend on how we see the hand of God in our problems. David's reaction to this particular problem was to run away (2 Sam.15:14). He made no defence because he saw no hope of victory. Why did this man of action give in so easily? Was it because he was disillusioned and depressed? Was it because he was old and tired? Was it because it was his son and friend who were conspiring against him and he had no stomach for such a fight? No, it was none of these things. David knew that all these events were part of God's judgement upon him because of his sin with Bathsheba. God had warned him: '"The sword shall never depart from your house, because you despised me and took the wife of Uriah the Hittite to be your own." This is what the Lord says: "Out of your own household I am going to bring calamity upon you. Before your very eyes I will take your wives and give them to one who is close to you, and he will lie with your wives in broad daylight. You did it in secret, but I will do this thing in broad daylight before all Israel"' (2 Sam. 12:10-12). Absalom was the one out of his own household, and Ahithophel was Bathsheba's grandfather. There was no doubt in David's mind why this was happening, so he did not resist what he saw as God's judgement.

Here we see a lovely spirit in David. Early in his life the same attitude was obvious when he was suffering for righteousness; now here it is again when he is suffering because of his own sin. As a martyr hounded by Saul, we can see the fruits of meekness, patience and confidence in

35

God as he refused to take revenge on Saul on the two occasions he had his enemy at his mercy. But here David is not sinned against, but the sinner. His sin has found him out, and he submissively bows his head and accepts the consequences.

There are times when as Christians we have to suffer for the sake of righteousness, but there are other times when our trials and problems are a direct result of our own sin. It is true that there is no eternal condemnation for the Christian, but that does not mean that God allows us to get away with sin. Sin brings consequences. It did for David and it will for us. What we are to learn from David is how to react when we know that God is dealing with us because of our sin.

David's reaction was twofold: he wept and he prayed. His weeping was not the tears of self-pity as, sadly, is often the case when Christians are caught out in their sin. The picture in 2 Samuel 15:30 reveals to us that these were tears of repentance: 'But David continued up the Mount of Olives, weeping as he went; his head was covered and he was barefoot.' A. W. Pink says of this, 'Throughout he is to be viewed as the humble penitent. God's rebuke was heavy upon him, and therefore did he humble himself beneath His mighty hand. Hence it is that we here see him giving outward expression to his self-abasement and grief for his sins, and for the miseries which he had brought upon himself, his family, and his people. Suitable tokens of his godly sorrow were these, for the covering of his head was a symbol of self-condemnation, while his walking barefooted betokened his mourning.'[2]

Repentance

True repentance will always lead to prayer, and some believe that it was in the midst of his tears of repentance upon the Mount of Olives that David wrote Psalm 3. To feel the consequences of sin without repentance will turn us in upon ourselves in despair and self-pity. This produces all sorts of different reactions in a Christian. We may feel bitter and critical of God. David could have thought that God was dealing too harshly with him. After all, the child who was the product of his sin with Bathsheba was dead. Surely that was enough punishment. And after the Bathsheba incident his repentance, as seen in Psalm 51, had been real and deep. Why were the consequences of that sin still arising? What believer has not experienced such thoughts at some time or other? Bitterness follows such a response and then, instead of repentance, we feel hard done by. It is God who is wrong, not us.

It may be that we feel confused. If the Bible says that there is no condemnation to those who are in Christ, and if we are told that God puts our sins behind his back and remembers them no more, and if Scripture teaches that the blood of Jesus Christ cleanses us from all sin — why is it that the consequences of sin are so real, so heavy and so painful?

God opposes sin with a pure, holy hatred, and he wants us to see it as he sees it. Sin is open rebellion against the character and law of God. It is a refusal to accept the authority and rule of God. It is bowing to the lordship of Satan and rejecting the lordship of Christ. In many ways sin in a believer is far worse than sin in an unbeliever.

There is no excuse for it because we are dead to sin (Rom. 6:11), we have been freed from sin's power (Rom. 6:6) and sin is no longer our master (Rom. 6:14). When the Christian sins, he is offering himself to sin to be used to promote wickedness (Rom. 6:13). That is terrible and we need to see it as such. It is true that there are no eternal consequences for the sin of the believer. Jesus took care of all that on the cross. But because God loves us, he will not allow us to get away with sin. If he did we would never take it as seriously as God does. We should hate sin because God hates it, but often we do not. So God shows us the evil of this rebellion by letting us feel here and now something of the consequences of sin. It is part of the teaching process that is seeking little by little to conform us to the mind of God.

Yet another reaction when we see the reality of our own sin is to stop praying. We feel too unworthy, too unclean, to come into the presence of God. The devil is eager to strengthen this feeling and keep us away from the Lord.

Prayer

If David felt any of these reactions, thankfully by the time he came to the Mount of Olives he was past them and he came humbly to God in prayer, with no confusion and no bitterness. The prayer of Psalm 3 is a beautiful reminder to us of how to approach God when we are suffering as a consequence of our own sin.

The consequences of sin

Firstly in verse 1, he faces up to the gravity of the situation. He is not deluding himself. There is no virtue in pretending everything is fine, when clearly it is not. We are not to whistle in the dark or pour out pious platitudes about the love of God. David, facing reality, spells out for us in verses 2-4 three important truths.

What the world says

The world says God will not help him. It is easy to understand this belief. After all, David is guilty. What is happening to him is only what God said would happen. Why should God help?

What the Christian knows

God does chastise his people, but only because he loves them. As Christians we should never forget this. Our dealings with God are always on the basis of grace, not merit. We deserve nothing, but God is always a shield around us. This is true even when our difficulties are of our own making.

What the Christian does

He prays; he cries to his God. We are never to despair as if there were no hope. Whether we are innocent or guilty in a particular situation, prayer is always to be our reaction.

The rest of the psalm is an example of true, believing

prayer. Here we see, in this terrible situation, David's confidence, trust, courage, dependence and assurance.

'He answers me,' says David in complete confidence (v. 4). This us not because we are good or bad but because our God is a loving Father and we are his children. Such confidence will produce the trust of verse 5. Worry and despair rob us of many things, including sleep, but the person trusting God sleeps in peace. The hymn-writer is correct when he wrote,

> Oh, what peace we often forfeit,
> Oh, what needless pain we bear,
> All because we do not carry
> Everything to God in prayer!

We really do get ourselves into a terrible mess if we refuse to trust God.

If confidence produces trust, then it is surely true that both produce courage. Thus David is able to say, 'I will not fear.' It is possible to pray and feel as miserable and fearful afterwards as we did before. This is because prayer is much more than just words. Prayer without a confidence and trust in God will not produce the courage that David exhibits in this psalm. When all three are present we shall know the sense of dependence David had upon God. 'Arise, O Lord! Deliver me, O my God', are the words of a man who had stopped trusting his own efforts. His eyes are now upon God. The whole sorry mess he was in came about because he took his eyes off God and let his lusts and desires rule him.

The whole process of believing prayer results in the assurance that 'From the Lord comes deliverance' (v. 8). God was chastising David, but this did not go on for ever. Eventually his enemies were routed and David was given back the throne. The lesson was needed. It was a hard time for this man of God but it was necessary. It always is.

5.
A poor man and his God —

David recalls the Lord's deliverance

When a person becomes a Christian he, or she, comes into a living and personal relationship with God. He is now a child of God and a member of the household of faith. The implications of this for that person's life are many and varied. But it does not mean that he never has any more problems or difficulties. Far from it. The experiences of God's people in Scripture show this. David speaks for us all when he wrote, 'A righteous man may have many problems' (Ps. 34:19).

This is so for several reasons. No Christian is sinless and often the repercussions of our sin cause us problems. Sometimes God has to teach us lessons that we will learn only in affliction, and therefore he allows trials to come into our lives. Then, of course, the devil is always seeking to make life difficult for God's people. So problems will come in all shapes and sizes. Therefore the question of most importance is, 'How do we cope with them?'

Psalm 34 is David's reaction to a major problem. The background to his problem is revealed in the introduction to the psalm, 'when he pretended to be insane before Abimelech'. This reference is to the incident in 1 Samuel 21. There is no mention in that chapter of Abimelech, but there is to Ahimelech, so it is easy to assume that they are the same man, but that would be wrong. Abimelech is a title for the Philistine kings, in much the same way as Pharaoh is used for the Egyptian kings. So in 1 Samuel 21 Abimelech is Achish, King of Gath. Ahimelech was a priest who was killed because of David's lies and deceit.

Lies and deceit

David was fleeing for his life from King Saul. When he came to Nob, he told Ahimelech the priest that he was on a secret mission for the king. The priest therefore helped David by giving him bread and Goliath's sword. David then moved on to Gath, a Philistine city, where he was recognized as a dangerous enemy. To escape punishment he pretended to be insane. Achish (Abimelech) therefore let him go free. The whole incident was unsavoury and degrading, but it did not end there. The priest, Ahimelech, together with eighty-four other men, was killed on Saul's orders for helping David — and all because of David's lies and deceit.

David must have been at an all-time spiritual low at this point, but even in such an awful spiritual condition he turns to God in this remarkable 34th Psalm. So often as Christians when pressures pile up, when our weaknesses overcome us and we feel hopeless failures, guilt makes us reluctant to pray. We convince ourselves that we must do something to rectify things before we can pray, and thus we deprive ourselves of the blessings of prayer by listening to the lies of Satan.

In our sin, in our failures, whatever the cause, there is only one place for the believer: 'This poor man called, and the Lord heard him; he saved him out of all his troubles' (v. 6). Psalm 34 was written some time after the incident in 1 Samuel 21. It is not the spontaneous cry of a soul in anguish, but David's considered, thought-out reflection as he looks back on the incident. It is a very carefully composed alphabetical psalm, with each of the twenty-two verses beginning with a consecutive letter of the Hebrew alphabet, *Aleph, Beth, Gimel*, etc. For this reason it is more valuable to us. David, coolly and calmly, looks back and wants us to learn from his mistakes. He says in verse 11, 'Come, my children, listen to me; I will teach you the fear of the Lord.'

This poor man

What makes a man poor? The first thing that springs to mind would be a lack of money, and this would have been true of David at the time. He was an outlaw, having to beg bread. It is true that his prospects were tremendous — he was chosen by God and the throne was to be his, but at that moment he was poor. All that being so, surely that is not what he meant in verse 6. He was a man after God's own heart, chosen, anointed, with glorious prospects, but in his troubles he did not behave as if these facts were so. He feared man and stooped to lies and deceit. There was no trust in God, and looking back David realizes how wrong he was. Compare Psalm 34:1,13 with the actual events in the presence of Achish. He is ashamed and feels himself to be a poor, miserable failure. This was his poverty.

Do you feel like this? You are a Christian, therefore your prospects are glorious. You love God but you do not always act as if it is so. You feel ashamed, a failure and a poor Christian. That may all be true; it certainly was of David, but David knew that if he was poor in his own estimation, he was righteous in God's. The same is true of all Christians. Our acceptance by God never depended upon our good deeds, therefore our bad deeds as Christians cannot lose that acceptance for us. Righteousness is a gift of God. It is a grace that comes to us through the gospel, 'For in the gospel a righteousness from God is revealed, a righteousness that is by faith' (Rom. 1:17). We are acceptable to God because of Christ's righteousness, not our own. This does not mean that we can treat sin lightly. Paul argues this out powerfully in Romans 6, and David in Psalm 34 clearly feels his spiritual poverty caused by his own sin. He is broken-hearted and crushed in spirit (v.18), but the Lord is close to such people. They are still God's people, therefore they can cry to the Lord for mercy and forgiveness.

When you feel so poor and begin to think you have no right to pray, remember your right does not depend upon your actions, but upon God's grace. When we are faithless God always remains faithful. He is rich in mercy even when we are poor in faith.

This poor man called

Because David was a man of God, certain things were inevitably to be seen in his life. They may have been shrouded by sin for a while but they would emerge again. And this is also true of every believer.

In verse 18 we see his deep conviction of sin; he was broken-hearted and crushed in spirit. For most of us conviction of sin is deeper for sins committed after conversion than anything we ever knew before we were saved. The man who can go on happily in his sin, denying it is wrong and justifying his evil deeds, is no child of God. The Christian is capable of just about any sin, but by the grace of God he will eventually see it for what it is and come back in repentance to the Lord.

Certain other things are also true of the Christian — the poor, guilty, failure of a Christian. He fears God (v. 7), trusts God (v. 8) and seeks God (v. 10). It is because these things are true of him that he will call out to God in his hopelessness and desperation. He does not politely petition: he calls, he cries. He is a failure; therefore it is a poor man's cry, depending on nothing in himself. But it is a powerful cry and is always effective because the Lord both hears and answers it.

The goodness of God

In the psalm our gaze is taken from the poor man to the infinite goodness of God. David reminds us that the Lord is attentive (v. 15); the Lord hears (v. 17); the Lord delivers (v. 17); the Lord is close (v. 18); the Lord saves (v. 18); the Lord delivers (v. 19); the Lord redeems (v. 22). What a God! He is worthy of our trust, our praise and our adoration. This is why David begins the psalm with three verses of delighting in the Lord.

It was not David's lies and deceit that got him out of his troubles, but the Lord. We have no need as Christians to resort to guile and deceit to avoid trouble. God is always to be our refuge and strength. The world's ways are not for God's people. They always dishonour God and make us spiritually poor.

Does God always hear and save us out of our troubles? He always hears but sometimes he tells us, as he did Paul in 2 Corinthians 12:7-10, 'I will not take your problem away but I will give you grace to cope with it.'

The consequence of such an answer for Paul was: 'I delight in weaknesses, in insults, in hardships, in persecutions, in difficulties. For when I am weak, then I am strong.'

Our problems may be as a result of our own sin, like David's in Psalm 34. They may be like Paul's, as part of God's dealing with us in grace. They may be a direct attack of the devil. Whichever is true, there is only one thing for the Christian to do — cry to God and look for his intervention.

Through all the changing scenes of life,
In trouble and in joy,
The praises of my God shall still
My heart and tongue employ.

A poor man and his God

O magnify the Lord with me,
With me exalt his name;
When in distress to him I called,
He to my rescue came.

The hosts of God encamp around
The dwellings of the just;
Deliverance he affords to all
Who on his succour trust.

(Nahum Tate and Nicholas Brady)

6.
Rest and conflict —

Asa relies on the Lord

Asa was one of the few good kings Israel or Judah had. Most were ungodly men who, by example and command, led the people away from God to worship idols. Asa was different, as is evident from 2 Chronicles 14:2-4: 'Asa did what was good and right in the eyes of the Lord his God. He removed the foreign altars and the high places, smashed the sacred stones and cut down the Asherah poles. He commanded Judah to seek the Lord, the God of their fathers, and to obey his laws and commands.'

As soon as he became king this man went into battle. It was a battle, not against the traditional enemies such as the Philistines or Midianites, but against the more powerful foes of sin and idolatry among the Lord's people. This was a real battle and it was one in which the Lord gave Asa the victory. The result was that for ten years there was peace with the other nations. God's people enjoyed a period of rest that was very unusual at that time, but it is an example of the biblical truth that righteousness exalts a nation.

When a nation, or a church, or an individual seeks to give the Lord his proper place in their lives, then the Lord honours this. Note in verse 6 that the peace they enjoyed was God-given and Asa understood this: 'We sought him and he has given us rest on every side' (2 Chron. 14:7). The Bible says there is no peace for the wicked. This means that the person who submits to sin and lives outside the love and grace of God will never know rest and peace of soul. He is forever in bondage, a slave to sin. His will is not free and his eyes are blind to the good things of God. He may prosper in terms of material possessions but he has no real rest.

An active rest

The Christian knows that rest is only found in Jesus. 'Come to me', the Saviour said, 'and I will give you rest.' But it is not the rest of indolence and laziness. We see in verse 7 that Asa used the rest to strengthen his defences. In the same way, the Christian realizes that to maintain the God-given rest he must be forever diligent to keep down the influence of sin in his life. Jesus must be Lord and King, and reign supreme in the heart. This involves constant communion with Christ in prayer and Bible study, and regular oneness and fellowship with the people of God. In this way we strengthen our defences.

There is to be no peace treaty with sin. The Christian fights against it and that fight takes place primarily in his heart and mind. Strangely, in this fight the peace and rest of God become more glorious and wondrous. This rest is not the rest of an armchair, neither is it a rest that makes the believer immune to outside pressures. Asa knew ten years of rest because the Lord gave it to him, but then in verse 9 we read that Zerah the Cushite came against him with a vast army. The Authorized Version tells us it was an army of a million men, one of the largest mentioned in Scripture.

Why did this happen? Was it that Asa had sinned and this was a punishment? There are no grounds in the context of the story to suggest this. Then why were this godly man and the people he had led back to God suddenly called upon to face an enemy stronger than anyone else had faced before? Obviously the Lord allowed this and he did so not as a punishment but as an encouragement, that they might learn more of his love and care for them, and thus discover an even deeper rest and peace.

Basic lessons

There is a tendency in most of us always to see difficulties as something terrible and not, as they sometimes are, as opportunities to discover new depths of God's love and provisions. There are basic spiritual lessons that we can never learn when things are going well. We need the problems and difficulties to teach us what real trust in the Lord is. They take our trust out of the realm of theory and into the hurly-burly of reality. There, all the impurities and deficiencies are burnt out and we are left with nothing but to look to God. It may not be a pleasant experience, but it can be and ought to be a spiritually enriching one.

Another lesson is that spiritual rest and blessing can be a dangerous thing. It is easy to slip into self-satisfaction, smugness and complacency. Look at Asa in verses 7 and 8. He had strong cities and a huge army. These were no tin soldiers but 580,000 brave fighting men. The king must have been proud of them and it would have been easy to rely upon them and to think that their strength was his security and the guarantee of peace. But then suddenly he is confronted with an army that is obviously superior to his, and his achievements look like vanishing in a moment.

In times of spiritual blessing in our lives, or in the life of our church, it is a temptation to sit back and feel secure, or even worse, to feel somewhat superior to other less fortunate saints. But if we open our eyes we shall see the strength of the enemy all around us. There is a vast army of sin and unbelief far more powerful than Zerah and, like Asa's enemy, just as determined to destroy us and to ruin all that God has done for us. There is nothing that infuriates Satan so much as a Christian or a church blessed by God.

Confidence in God

So what do we do? We follow Asa's example. He knew that to sit and wait would be fatal, so he went out to meet the enemy. He could have thought he would wait until he was stronger and better prepared, but he knew that he would never be strong enough, and anyway the battle was now, not next year, so he faced the problem head on. However it was not an act of folly; rather it was an act of faith. We read, 'Then Asa called to the Lord his God and said, "Lord, there is no one like you to help the powerless against the mighty. Help us, O Lord our God, for we rely on you, and in your name we have come against this vast army. O Lord, you are our God; do not let man prevail against you"' (2 Chron. 14:11).

Is not Asa's God our God? Is not the God who helped Moses and Elijah, Luther and Calvin, Whitefield and Spurgeon our God? It is not more men or more money we need, but more calling upon God, more imploring his help. We are told to 'approach the throne of grace with confidence, so that we may receive mercy and find grace to help us in our time of need' (Heb. 4:16). David in Psalm 20 speaks with the same confidence,

> Now I know that the Lord saves his anointed;
>   he answers him from his holy heaven
>   with the saving power of his right hand.
> Some trust in chariots and some in horses,
>   but we trust in the name of the Lord our God
>   (Ps. 20:6-7).

Asa had learnt from his dealings with the Lord that confidence in God was most reasonable. There is no one like God to help the powerless. Do we believe that? Then should we not have the same confidence? Such confidence creates a simplicity in prayer. Asa does not waste time telling God all the details of the size of the armies. He just says, 'Lord they are mighty; we are powerless. Help us.' It was so simple. You don't need a degree in theology to pray like that. You don't need to have a silver tongue. The prayer was simple but powerful because the Lord loves to help his people in their needs.

The relationship of the Christian to his God is not a complex one of rituals, ceremonies and liturgies. It is simply a relationship of Father and child. So, 'Help us,' is most natural and appropriate.

Asa's prayer continues, 'We rely on you.' This is the only way for a Christian to face difficulties. We cannot rely upon our knowledge, or ability, or experience, or numbers. We rely only upon the Lord. We do not say, 'Lord look at our talents and abilities, and please use them.' We say, 'Lord without you we have nothing, no power, no chance. Help us, Lord, for we have no one else.' It is in the Lord's name we face the enemies that seek to pull us down, not in the name of some preacher or church. The name that is above all names, the name that causes devils to tremble and hell to shake, is the name of Jesus.

The last petition in the prayer puts all our difficulties into a proper context: 'Do not let man prevail against you.' Asa knew the battle was not merely Zerah versus Asa, but the powers of darkness against God. God's glory was at stake. When we realize this it will totally change our attitude to the difficulties that invade our lives. It will take away the fear that stems from thinking that it all depends on us. This will be replaced by a sense of excitement and anticipation. We shall expect to see God at work. Then the battle becomes a privilege, something not to fear, but to face confidently in the strength which God supplies.

7.
Facing the seemingly impossible —

David and Goliath

Often in the Christian life the thing that causes us to
struggle most is the awareness of our own inadequacy.
We are called upon to engage in battles against enemies
that seem to possess far more resources and power than
we do. Thus the impossible stares us in the face and not
only do we struggle, but often we just give up. We are
aware of the story of David and Goliath (1 Sam. 17) but
it may seem rather unreal to us and we cannot see
ourselves in the rôle of a David. If that is the case then we
are missing the main lesson of the story. David gained the
victory over Goliath for one reason only — his total and
uncompromising trust in the Lord. All Christians are
called upon to demonstrate such trust and it is not un-
reasonable or misplaced.

The giant

The Israelites and Philistines were once more lined up in
battle. There was nothing new about that; what was new
this time was the presence of Goliath. This man was huge.

He was over nine feet, or about three metres, tall. The Bible describes in detail the fearsome sight that confronted the people of God (2 Sam.17: 4-7). They were terrified, but even worse than the sight of Goliath was his challenge to single combat (vv. 8-9). This giant was brimming with confidence. He could see no way in which he could lose, so he defiantly challenged the people of God.

The Israelites were in total agreement with Goliath. They were mesmerized by his size and saw no way anyone could defeat him.

So no one would take up the challenge, yet in their midst was Jonathan who with his armour-bearer had killed twenty Philistines. And King Saul himself was a very big man, head and shoulders taller than any other Israelite. The sad fact was that God's people had sunk to the level of the pagan and thought only in terms of physical size and strength. God was forgotten. The challenge of Goliath was not taken up because he seemed to them to be invincible.

The giants of today are also shouting their challenges to God's people. They too are very confident in their own strength and power. Unbelief ridicules the Bible. Permissiveness laughs at Christian morality. These combine with challenges in our lives to witness, to evangelize, to pray, and we think, 'What is the use of trying? We cannot win.' We tremble before such giants and God is forgotten.

This is all very relevant for us today. The challenges are great. Are we overcome by the seeming power of the opposition? Are we being paralysed by fear into activity? Do we believe that God is helpless before such enemies?

Fear forgets

The challenge was put off for forty days. But soon it had to be faced. Someone must fight, but they had no one to match Goliath's size, and worse than that, they had no one with the courage to try. Smaller had been known to defeat bigger, but if there is no heart for the battle then victory becomes impossible.

The problem with God's people was that their fear had led them to forget their own history. They forgot Gideon and Barak and Samson, who through faith had subdued kingdoms. When Christians forget their history they are in serious trouble. Our history is a reminder of what God has done and is the greatest possible deterrent to a paralysing fear. The one Israelite who was not frightened by the giant was the man who remembered what God had done. David was confident, not because he was a silly and arrogant youth, but because 'The Lord who delivered me from the paw of the lion and the paw of the bear will deliver me from the hand of this Philistine' (1 Sam. 17:37). He had proved God and therefore no giant was invincible. With Almighty God on his side how could he possibly feel inadequate?

When we as Christians have to face seemingly invincible opposition, it is perfectly correct that we have no confidence in ourselves, but if we have proved God in previous battles then we know that we can have confidence in him. You may not have had to fight lions or bears like David, but there have been other battles, there have been previous crises. Did God let you down?

Have you proved God in the hottest battle of all — in prayer? The greatest battles of our faith are not fought out in the world, but on our knees. These are fought alone with no human help. There the enemy attacks us ruthlessly and that is why prayer is so hard. But if we know the victory in secret prayer we shall not taste defeat when we meet the enemy in public.

David remembered what God had done for him and this was the only reason he volunteered to fight Goliath. He refused Saul's armour and took what appeared to be the most ridiculous of weapons. But David was not going against this giant with merely a sling and five stones, but in the name of the Lord. He said to the Philistine, 'You come against me with a sword and spear and javelin, but I come against you in the name of the Lord Almighty, the God of the armies of Israel, whom you have defied' (1 Sam. 17:45).

We need to ask ourselves if we believe that our resources are the resources of heaven? Do we believe that if God is for us none can be against us? Do we believe that one with God is a majority? The answers to these questions will determine how we face today's giants of unbelief.

The result seemed inevitable

No one gave David a hope of victory. His brother Eliab said he was conceited (v. 28), Saul said he was too inexperienced (v. 33), Goliath despised him (vv. 41-44), but David knew that the battle was the Lord's (v. 47).

Facing the seemingly impossible

So often Christians are put off by what seems to be inevitable. We feel we have no hope of success, so we do not try. In our churches we often resign ourselves to defeat and smaller congregations and dwindling Sunday Schools and continuing financial difficulties. All these are regarded as inevitable. But nothing is inevitable other than the ultimate triumph of Christ. Much today could be changed by a faith like David's coupled with a courage to trust God. The lessons from the story of David and Goliath are crucial for us today.

The giant seemed to have all the advantages of size, strength and weapons. David took what was available to all, five stones, but he trusted God and slew Goliath with the giant's sword. In many ways Goliath was a big sham. He was dressed to frighten, but his size would have made him slow and clumsy. A big, strong, clever man like Saul should have been able to defeat him easily. But God's people were beaten by an outward show of arrogance.

This was not an impossible achievement by David. It required courage and trust, but it was perfectly possible. God did not work a miracle for his servant to gain the victory. All the ingredients of success were there for the man who would trust God. And the giants of today can be toppled with the same combination of courage and faith. The history of the Christian church is full of it. God is still on the throne. The devil and his servants live a lie, a sham, a bluff. It is time we started calling the bluff and triumphing for God.

8.
Asked to do the impossible —

Ezekiel and the dry bones

Ezekiel's vision of the valley of dry bones (Ezek. 37) is a remarkable story. But it is only meant to convey to us a truth from God. This is made clear in verse 11: 'These bones are the whole house of Israel.' It was a picture of a people who had lost all hope. Defeat, despair and depression were the order of the day.

Deadness

As a result of the activity of the Holy Spirit in a way and manner we cannot understand, Ezekiel found himself in the middle of a valley filled with dead men's bones. We are told in verse 2 that the bones were very dry — the men had been dead for a long time. This was no recent disaster but the end product of a long process of death and decay. The valley was full of bones — it was a total disaster, not merely something affecting a few.

How did the prophet feel as he saw this? Did he experience shock and revulsion? Was he sickened? The vision was meant by God to hit him hard and we can be assured that it did. God led him to and fro in this graveyard to let the whole scene sink into the prophet's mind, and then God asked him a question, 'Can these bones live?', followed by a command: 'Prophesy to these bones.'

Does history, sacred or secular, offer a more ridiculous picture than this? Here is the height of hopelessness. Who ever had such a dumb congregation? Before Ezekiel, Isaiah has seen his nation in terrible spiritual sickness, but now the sickness had turned to death and the dead bones offered only despair. Written over the scene in large capital letters is the word 'impossibility'.

The valley of dry bones speaks of the spiritual condition of the nation — our nation. Do we see it as God does? Is God showing us the true spiritual condition of men and women in our nation? Like Ezekiel, we pass to and fro among the people every day, but do we see and feel the situation? Jesus did, and he wept over Jerusalem. Paul did, and he longed for Israel to be saved. John Elias did in the Wales of 1841: 'They walk in darkness, without knowing whither they go; and the ministry leaves them in that condition. Oh, how sad! God, no doubt, is hiding himself! There is strength, light and warmth wherever his gracious presence is found. Oh, that he would return to us, for his name's sake! Oh, that he would turn to revive us! We have deserved this on account of our great iniquities, but he can visit us in his grace. Oh, that I might see one gracious and powerful divine visitation, in Anglesey, before I sleep in death!'[3] If we see our nation like this, do we despair? Do we feel it is all impossible?

Faith

It is at this point that faith must take over. No faith is needed to do the possible. Again and again God asks men to do, not what they can, but what they cannot do. God's dealings with us are not intended to show us how clever we are if only we will try, but rather that there are situations that confront us sometimes in which, no matter how hard we try, we are helpless. This was not like David and Goliath. This was no arrogant show. These men were dead. Yet Ezekiel was commanded to preach to them.

The prophet was led by the Spirit into this situation and he must have shuddered at the sight of mile after mile of dry bones. Many would have run away, but not this man. His eyes were on God and his ears were opened to the voice of God. He said, 'So I prophesied as I was commanded' (v. 7). Ezekiel stood before this scene of deadness and said, 'Dry bones, hear the word of the Lord!' Was his action madness, or faith? Heaven knew it was not madness because heaven knew the power of God. But if the world could have viewed this amazing scene, it would have locked the prophet away, condemned as insane. If many religious people had seen it, they would have accused Ezekiel of cheapening the gospel and bringing the church into disrepute. Ezekiel was willing to become a fool for Christ's sake. He just did exactly what God told him. He said to bones that had no ears, 'Hear the word of the Lord!'

What would we have done? Very often we are all too prone, in order to save face, to modify God's commands.

We reason and rationalize when the situation is so desperate that it calls for nothing but obedience. And we are always the losers. But Ezekiel did exactly as he was told and God worked the impossible.

Can these bones live?

Before God did the impossible he asked the prophet a very important question: 'Can these bones live?' The purpose of the question was to ascertain Ezekiel's response to God and what was being shown him. If anyone else had asked the question, his answer would promptly have been, 'No, it is impossible.' But it is God who is asking, so he answers, 'Sovereign Lord, you alone know.' The answer tells us much about this man.

He believed in a sovereign God. He did not merely hold to a doctrine of divine sovereignty, but actually believed in the reality and practicality of this great truth. He believed in a God of power who is able to do the impossible; therefore he was not unduly pessimistic. The doctrine of God's sovereignty should be a sweet and blessed comfort in hopeless and impossible situations. Neither was he unduly optimistic. He did not say, as he looked at that terrible valley, that they were going to see a great harvest of souls. That would have been too glib and would have smacked of evangelical jargon. All he said was, 'O Sovereign Lord, you alone know.' In effect he was saying, 'Lord, if it can be done, you alone must do it.' All things are possible to our God.

Notice that divine sovereignty is linked inevitably to divine omniscience — 'You know.' God knows because he ordains and plans. And sometimes, to encourage his people, God reveals in advance to them what he is about to do. He did so for the prophet. In the previous chapter there is a lovely description of what God is going to do for these dry bones: 'I will sprinkle clean water on you, and you will be clean; I will cleanse you from all your impurities and from all your idols. I will give you a new heart and put a new spirit in you; I will remove from you your heart of stone and give you a heart of flesh. And I will put my Spirit in you and move you to follow my decrees and be careful to keep my laws' (Ezek. 36: 25-27).

As we look at the spiritual decadence and deadness of our nation, do we despair? Do we think that things have deteriorated so much that the people are beyond redemption? Perhaps God is saying to us, 'Can these bones live? Can such dead souls be saved?' Your godless relatives, that blaspheming foul-mouthed man at work, those awkward neighbours, those pleasant, lovely folk you know who have no time for God — can such as these be saved?

If we are beginning to have a real spiritual burden for these people, isn't that God's doing? And isn't that a ground for optimism, not pessimism? You can be sure that if God is showing us these things he is also saying to us, 'Preach to these bones. Tell them my gospel, and tell it with the confidence of Ezekiel when he says, "I will make breath enter you, and you will come to life. I will attach tendons to you and make flesh come upon you and cover you with skin; I will put breath in you, and you will come to life"' (Ezek. 37:5-6). Are we going to be like Ezekiel? 'So I prophesied as I was commanded.' God's commands are not to be questioned or debated but obeyed. No doubt he felt rather awkward preaching to dead bones. Perhaps he was embarrassed, but he did it. Often we feel inadequate in witnessing to sinners. Good! That is the best qualification because it safeguards us from trusting in our own abilities and throws us entirely upon the Lord. Remember, God is never inadequate. Our business is to obey. God will do the rest.

9.
Inheriting a situation —

Haggai calls the people to work

We have seen that the struggles of the Christian life are very real. Sometimes the problems are of our own making, the product of our sin, but it is also true that sometimes we inherit difficulties. Few would argue that many of the church's problems of today are the result of the neglect and indolence of previous generations. Liberal theology, materialism and nominal church-going have over the years led to the decline of Christianity that we struggle against today. That does not mean that we can feel complacent and argue that it is not our fault. Today's Christians are called to minister to today's situation, and even though many of our problems are inherited they still have to be faced and dealt with.

Haggai inherited a condition of awful spiritual neglect and how he set about dealing with it is an example for us. In the year 536 B.C. the Persian emperor Cyrus permitted the Jewish exiles to return to Jerusalem to rebuild the temple. About 50,000 returned and with great zeal and effort they set about their task. We read of this in the book of Ezra. One of the first things they did was to take up an offering to finance the work (Ezra 2:69). It has been calculated that in today's terms this was over two million pounds sterling. That was the measure of their earnestness, and in a very short time they had laid the foundation of the temple.

Then difficulties arose. Cyrus died, there was opposition from the Samaritans and the work stopped. For about fifteen years little or nothing was done, and then in 520 B.C. God sent Haggai to confront the people with their distorted priorities. 'This is what the Lord Almighty says: "These people say, 'The time has not yet come for the Lord's house to be built.'"' Then the word of the Lord came through the prophet Haggai: "Is it a time for you yourselves to be living in your panelled houses, while this house remains a ruin?" Now this is what the Lord Almighty says: "Give careful thought to your ways. You have planted much, but have harvested little. You eat, but never have enough. You drink, but never have your fill. You put on clothes, but are not warm. You earn wages, only to put them in a purse with holes in it"' (Hag. 1:2-5).

The people were disillusioned and frustrated. Their hopes and expectations were shattered. The great days of the past, when they counted for something, were gone, and all that was left was a temple in ruins, problems on all sides and no real hope of ever accomplishing anything. Doesn't all this sound amazingly like our day? Gone are the big congregations and packed churches. We are in a post-Christian era. Like them we are only a remnant but God has given us a task. There is also another similarity that has to be noted. Their original zeal had gone. They had got caught up in their own pursuits and their God-given task was forgotten. How true this is of so many of today's people of God! Twenty years ago their zeal for the Lord's work knew no bounds. They gave unstintingly of their time and money, but not now. Other things, legitimate things, have taken priority and they have left the burden of God's work to others.

This was the situation that Haggai inherited. He did not create it but he had to deal with it. His message to the people is to *think*. Twice, in verses 5 and 7, he urges them to give careful thought to their situation. In verse 6, we have a vivid picture of a dissatisfied man, and this is not the man of the world, but a picture of a materially-minded child of God whose priorities are all wrong.

Sadly this picture is too accurate for comfort in describing many of today's Christians. Dissatisfaction and disillusionment seem to characterize so many modern believers. They sing, 'And now I am happy all the day,' but they are not. They delight to proclaim, 'None but Christ can satisfy,' but they are not satisfied. Why is this so? What is the problem? These Christians will give all sorts of answers, but there is only one real issue here. The problem is the Christian's relationship with, and commitment to, the Lord. We seem to have lost our way, lost our expectations, lost our zeal and lost our first love. The answer is to think, to consider, to ponder on where we are spiritually. When we do that we shall see that there is only one way out of the dilemma — to turn back to God.

That is exactly the message of Haggai. What we need

is a clearer vision of the greatness and glory of God, and a correspondingly greater commitment to him. Haggai proceeds to remind the people of basic truths about God.

God's pleasure (1:8)

We must stop doing things in the vague hope that they may please God and do them in the sure knowledge that God will be pleased. This means learning from Scripture what God expects from us.

In Ephesians 5:10 Paul urges the Christians to 'find out what pleases the Lord', and this is in the context of what it means to live a Christ-centred, God-honouring life. God's pleasure should be our top priority.

God's preacher (1:12-13)

If we acknowledge, as Israel did of Haggai, that the preacher is sent by God, then we must listen to him, because his authority is not in his personality or oratory, but in the fact that God has sent him. This does not mean that he is infallible, but you must be careful that you do not reject his message merely because it does not suit you. This attitude to the Word of God preached to us produces a healthy fear of the Lord.

God's presence (1:13)

'I am with you,' is the greatest possible encouragement we can have. The work is hard; there is little response to the gospel and we may be tempted to pack it all in. But God says, 'I am with you.' This is the only guarantee of blessing — but what a guarantee! If God is with us it does not matter who is against us. But we shall only know God's presence when we do his pleasure and recognize his voice through his sent preachers. This awareness transforms spiritual pigmies into giants and reduces mountains to molehills.

God's purposes (2:3)

Haggai 2:3 is a wonderful reminder that God's purposes are always fulfilled even though the situation may appear to be hopeless. The temple they were building would, according to the earlier prophets, surpass Solomon's temple in glory and splendour, but it all appeared totally improbable. The wise old heads who could remember the former glories probably dismissed the present work as a waste of time. Such pessimism is still with us, but God says, 'The glory of this present house will be greater than the glory of the former house' (2:9). To lose sight of God, or doubt his purposes, means certain defeat, but to believe and hold onto these brings a holy boldness and a desire to work.

God's promises (2:4-5)

These are the covenant promises made when the nations came out of Egypt. The essence of the promises was that God's Spirit would remain among his people. We need

73

again to hear that promise and believe it. This is a great incentive to work, to be strong and not to fear. It is not our work but God's, so in spite of all the struggles stick at it and look for and expect God to work.

God's power (2:6-7)

These verses remind us of the unsurpassed power of God. Who can withstand such a God? And it is to him that we are to look: a God who is able and willing to bless his people. In the work of such a God there is no cause for doubt or depression. If today's struggles are a reality, so too will tomorrow's victories be. He will fill his house with glory. Nothing is more sure than this.

10.
Concern for the church —

Isaiah's prayer for Zion

In chapter 62 of his book we find Isaiah deeply concerned
for the condition of Zion, of Jerusalem. He sees immense
problems confronting the people that will bring disgrace
and humiliation. His concern is not just a sentimental one.
Zion is the city of God. Jerusalem is the city of the great
King. So God's glory is involved here. The prophet is so
concerned that he feels he must do something about it. He
says, 'I will not keep silent ... I will not remain quiet' until
the situation changes.

Jesus quoted from this section of Isaiah in Luke 4 and
applied it to the church and to gospel days. Commenting
on this, Dr Lloyd-Jones said, 'This is a call to the church
in a time of declension, in a time when she is beset by
enemies and problems. So we can take this picture today
and apply it to ourselves.'[4]

The church in trouble

Zion is often in Scripture a picture of the church. That is
why so many hymns speak of Zion when referring to the

church. The prophet is concerned for Zion and today there are many folk concerned for their church. They have a concern for a leaky roof and the need to raise thousands of pounds for repairs. This is a legitimate concern but it was not Isaiah's concern. His thought was not on the fabric, architecture, art treasures or culture of Zion, but on its spiritual poverty, particularly the oppression that dominated the people of God. They were deserted and desolate.

Isaiah was under no illusion. He saw the problem and he saw the reason. A lesser man would have given all sorts of explanations for the sorry state of God's people, but the prophet knew there was only one. He spells it out in 64:6-7: they were under the judgement of God because of their sin.

Do we see how applicable this is to us today? We sing, 'Glorious things of thee are spoken, Zion city of our God.' But that is not true any more. No one says glorious things of today's church. We too are deserted and desolate, and for the same reason as Isaiah points out. Does this concern us? Do we feel like this man, that we are not prepared to accept the situation, and want to do something about it?

What the church is

Why was Isaiah not prepared to accept things as they were? Most Christians seem to be! What is the reason for his insistence that he will not rest until there is a change? Why, if as he says, Zion was under the judgement of God, does he not also say, 'There is nothing that can be done'?

Because here was a man who really knew what the church is. In verse 3 he gives a remarkable description of the people of God: 'You will be a crown of splendour in the Lord's hand, a royal diadem in the hand of your God.'

The church is the masterpiece of God, the greatest beauty on earth. She is the glorious crown of God's majesty — a crown not resting on his head as an ornament to be admired, but as a tool in his hand to be used for his glory. The church, he says in verse 1, has a righteousness and brightness that need to shine out into the world. It is because Isaiah sees the church as she is meant to be, and sees her present sorry condition, that he feels so deeply that he must do something. He cannot and will not accept the situation. He is not just looking back and lamenting what was but is no longer. On the contrary, he is looking forward to what can be and will be — verse 3 is in the future tense.

The question is often asked, 'Has the church any future?' Yes, says this man, a future as bright as the glory of God. The two names in verse 4 bring before us his great confidence. 'Hephzibah' means, 'God delights in her,' and 'Beulah' means, 'married to God'. This is in perfect accord with the New Testament picture of the church as the bride of Christ. Isaiah does not see the church as a widow whose husband is dead and whose best and happiest days are all in the past. In verse 5, he sees the church as a young virgin bride whose future is glorious because her husband, the living God, delights in her and rejoices over her. For this reason, he sees the church influencing the world. The nations and powers of the world will see her righteousness and glory (v. 2). This is the church. It is not some pathetic little group of nobodies, but a crown of splendour and a royal diadem in the hand of God.

Isaiah sees all this and longs for it. Do you? Do you see the church like this? Do you long for the better days of Hephzibah and Beulah? Then what can we do? We can start by following the prophet's example.

A holy restlessness

His spirit begins to agitate and there is a holy restlessness in his soul. No one has ever done anything of any significance in the service of God without first of all a holy restlessness. This is the exact opposite of sitting at ease in Zion.

He is not discontent with God and he is not disillusioned. He is beginning to see things clearly. Isaiah sees the mess the church is in and he sees the reason for this, but he does not blame others. All God's people are at fault. If he was to fall into the devil's trap of blaming others he would never have felt so deeply the concern expressed here. This holy restlessness drives him to do something. But what?

Watchmen

He posts watchmen on the walls of Jerusalem (v. 6). Their function was to warn of the enemy's approach and prepare the people for battle. So often in the Old Testament the problem was that God's people had welcomed the enemy, and with the enemy had come their gods. This had led to idolatry and consequently God's anger on them and ultimately to the mess they were now in.

For us today this means a concern for the truth of God and an unwillingness to compromise with false doctrine and sinful living. It is a departure from biblical truth that causes the problem for the church. But it is no use saying, 'I believe in the truth of Scripture,' and then failing to apply that truth in our own personal lives. Nothing will change until we do this, but it is not enough. There is also something else we must do.

Prayer

In verses 6 and 7 Isaiah tells us to give ourselves no rest and give God no rest until he comes and changes things. He is talking of persistent, continual, urgent prayer. No stopping 'until ...' reminds us of Jacob at Peniel: 'I will not let you go unless you bless me' (Gen. 32:26). Jesus sets the same example before us in the parables in Luke 11 and 18 of the friend at midnight and the woman and the unjust judge.

What are we to pray for?

For the church to be again a crown of splendour and a royal diadem in God's hand.

For the world to see the righteousness and glory of God.

For the new names of Hephzibah and Beulah

For the church to be what God meant it to be.

11.
A man in a hurry —

Nehemiah and the rebuilding of Jerusalem

Nehemiah came to Jerusalem about seventy years after
Haggai. By then the temple had been rebuilt but there
were other problems for the Jews. They were 'in great
trouble and disgrace. The wall of Jerusalem is broken
down, and its gates have been burned with fire' (Neh.
1:3). It was this sorry situation that brought Nehemiah to
Jerusalem. He lived in the city of Susa, hundreds of miles
from Jerusalem, working as the cupbearer to the Persian
king, Artaxerxes. His life was fairly comfortable and
trouble-free, but when he heard of the plight of his fellow
Jews, he was deeply grieved and felt he must help them.

As the story of this remarkable man unfolds, we see
that his first concern was to rebuild the broken walls of the
city. The defence and security of the people depended
upon the strength of the walls, so this was no misplaced
priority. If ever there was a right man for the job it was
Nehemiah. He was a great leader, a superb organizer and
a born motivator of men. He took on a task that had
languished for years and got it done in fifty-two days. He
was a man of courage and vision, and could face his

enemies and declare, 'I am carrying on a great project and cannot go down. Why should the work stop while I leave it and go down to you?' (6:3).

Commendable though these qualities are, they were not the reasons that made Nehemiah so useful in God's service. A Christian could have all these and yet be totally useless in the work of the Lord. The things that made Nehemiah so effective for God were his passion and deep feeling and his sense of identity with the need and suffering of God's people. When he heard of their tragic circumstances, his reaction of mourning and fasting and praying showed the sort of man he was. Such men can be difficult for other Christians to cope with because they are always in a hurry. Once the burden is felt and the vision caught, the work has to be done. Many a fine saint, taking on a similar task to that faced by Nehemiah, would allow himself a two- or three-year plan to achieve it. Nehemiah did it in fifty-two days!

No delay

This was not a man, all heart and no brains, rushing in like a fool. The first thing he did was to sit down — to weep, to mourn, to fast and to pray. This lasted from the month Kislev to the month Nisan, that is for four months. But once the vision of what God wanted him to do was caught, there was no holding him back.

It is often said that God is never in a hurry and of course there is truth in that because the Lord does not work to a clock or a calendar. But none the less there are times when

A man in a hurry

Scripture urges speed and no delay. It does so, for instance, in the realm of salvation, Today, not tomorrow, is the day of salvation. There are times in the lives of God's people when we cannot afford the luxury of dither and delay. Nehemiah's days were such a time — the walls were down, the city was defenceless and something had to be done at once.

Surely our own days are similar. The state of biblical Christianity in our land is so deplorable that delay while we debate the niceties of procedure and order is not on. There is a job to be done and we ought to be getting on with it. There are some believers so afraid of doing the wrong thing that they fail to do anything. Others are afraid speed will bring in error and so again nothing is done to face the real problems of today. We have become very skilful at setting up committees and very useless at actually doing anything.

Nehemiah did not waste time setting up a committee to decide how high the walls should be — fifteen foot or twenty foot; they were down, so the need was to get them up again. He did not debate what colour they would paint the gates when they were built; they were burnt and needed to be repaired. So often debates, some on important issues but many on trivial ones, seem to frustrate action. We talk and talk and talk, while souls are going to hell without ever hearing the gospel. Our failure to reach our nation with the gospel is the great need of today. The shallowness of evangelicalism and the worldliness of so many Christians today are a scandal. These are the issues that need to be addressed, and addressed seriously and urgently.

Nehemiah's timetable

Nehemiah was working to a timetable set him by King Artaxerxes (Neh. 2:6). But we have to say that a greater King than the Persian was directing this man. Nehemiah's timetable is interesting. It shows a man in a hurry but not neglecting the crucial matter of prayer and seeking God.

Praying and seeking God's help	4 months
Getting King Artaxerxes to help	1 hour??
In Jerusalem getting first-hand experience of the problem	3 days
A detailed examination of the problem (2:12)	1 night
The work itself	52 days

The work itself was hard and the personal sacrifice involved was great. They worked day and night and did not even take their clothes off (4:21-23). There were inward problems of rich Jews taking advantage of poorer ones (Neh. 5). Also there were the outside pressures from men like Sanballat and Tobiah (Neh. 6). There was even personal slander against Nehemiah (6:6-7). All this God's servant took in his stride. He had a great work to do, and he did it.

What God wants from us

What is it that God wants from us in our day and age?

A man in a hurry

Christians of passion and feeling

Whatever gifts we may or may not have, without passion and feeling we shall be useless in God's service. How do you react to the weakness of the church and to the spiritual needs of today? When Nehemiah heard of the difficulties he did not shrug them off as to be expected and beyond hope. The problem drove him to God in contemplation and prayer. His sitting down in Nehemiah 1:4 was not an act of indifference, because he sat down and wept. But it was not the weeping of despair, because he also fasted and prayed.

Are you concerned about our nation? Then do you weep and pray? If we mourn for the spiritual state of our people and do not pray, it is an act of despair. If we pray but do not weep, it is an act of formality with no real concern. But if we pray and weep, it is an act of faith and hope.

Christians who are willing to get involved

Nehemiah heard of a problem that was hundreds of miles away. He could have said it was nothing to do with him. Compared to other Jews he was well off, with a good job and sheltered from the sort of problems he heard of. He was privileged, but privilege, especially God-given privilege, brings with it responsibility. It is easy to forget this and retire into a little cocoon and forget others. Often with Christians prosperity, whether spiritual or material, blunts a sense of concern. Not so Nehemiah. He got involved.

Struggling but winning

Are we prepared to get involved and do something about the godlessness of today? The church has too many spectators who come only to watch and do nothing. This is sometimes caused by indifference, sometimes by bad leadership, which frustrates vision and effort. Whatever the reason, it is not good enough. We all need to get involved by earnest prayer and bold witness and hard work.

Christians with a vision of what can be done and who are willing to get on with it

The days are desperate, and urgency, not complacency, is needed. Nehemiah took risks for God. His action in coming before the king with a sad face could have cost him his life. The Bible is full of risk-takers, men and women who were willing to follow God, no matter what the cost.

Elijah pouring water on a sacrifice he wanted to see burnt was such a risk-taker. So too was Peter getting out of the boat to walk on the water. And what about Moses striking a rock to obtain water, or Ezekiel preaching to dead bones? These were not reckless and silly men but men with a vision of the glory and power of God, men who believed things could be changed and sought to change them. They struggled against opposition as well as against their own uncertainties but they kept their eye on the Lord and the victory they won was all due to his love and grace.

12.
Jehovah, great I AM —

The God who is with us

'Struggling but winning' would sum up the lives of most of the people of God both in biblical times and ever since. The Christian life is no bed of roses, but it is one in which we can expect to know the help of God. We are not left on our own to cope as best we can; the Lord in Scripture makes numerous promises to guide, to help and to provide for his people. One of the most thrilling promises for the struggling saint is found in Isaiah 43:2:

> When you pass through the waters,
>   I will be with you;
> and when you pass through the rivers,
>   they will not sweep over you.
> When you walk through the fire,
>   you will not be burned;
>   the flames will not set you ablaze.

Such promises are only valuable to us because of the one who makes them. Any fool can make promises he cannot keep, but this promise is made by the one who says, 'I am the Lord, your God, the Holy One of Israel, your Saviour' (Isa. 43:3). It is one thing to have a great promise made to us but quite another for us to claim it and know the reality and fulfilment of it. The secret of the men we have studied in this book was that such promises were not theory but experience for them, and this was because they had a high view of the God they served. They knew God, loved God, believed God and trusted God.

Expectancy

There is nothing more important in the Christian life than our understanding of who God is. This will govern everything we do and particularly our sense of expectancy. Take, for instance, the promise in Isaiah 43:2. There God is promising that in the fires of affliction and the waters of sorrow, he will be with us to ensure that these struggles do not overwhelm us. The Lord made that promise 2,700 years ago, but is it relevant to us today? Do we believe God can still minister to us like that, and do we expect him to? Is God still God?

Every evangelical Christian would without hesitation say 'Yes'. We are believers. We believe the Bible. We believe God will bless us. But is Tozer right when he wrote, 'We are believers and we can quote the creed with approval. We believe it, but we believe that God will bless some other people, some other place, some other time — but not now, not here and not us'?[5] This basically is our problem, and, to quote Tozer again, 'If we allow the gloomy voice of unbelief to whisper to us that God will bless some other time but not now, some other place but not here, some other people but not us, we might as well turn off the lights because nobody will get anywhere.'[6]

However, there is another voice that calls for our attention. The voice of faith says that God means what he says. What he did, he can still do. God is still the same God as he was in Bible times.

Which voice do we listen to? The answer to that will determine the sort of Christian lives we live. It will determine the depth of our Christian experience and the breadth of our vision and expectancy. All the men we have looked at, Moses, Gideon, Asa, David and the rest, had the same battle with faith and unbelief. Anything they experienced and accomplished that was of any value was when the voice of faith triumphed.

Faith is most reasonable. It is not a step into the dark but a step out of the dark into the light of God. It hears the promise of God, believes it and trusts God. It is the character of God that makes faith so reasonable.

The LORD

You will notice that in Isaiah 43 and in much of the Old Testament the name LORD is in capital letters. This means that the Hebrew word used was *Yahweh*. This was the name by which God revealed himself to Moses in the burning bush when he said, 'I AM WHO I AM.' The old Hebrew people came to believe that the name *Yahweh* was too sacred to pronounce, so another word for the Lord was used, *Adonai.* When this was written they combined the vowels of *Adonai* with the consonants *Yahweh* to give 'Jehovah'. Dr Packer says, 'The meaning of Yahweh is that which was symbolized by the flame in the bush which did not need to feed on the wood of the bush. Yahweh signifies an inexhaustible ruler — God of limitless life and power — a God, therefore, whom it is safe to trust at all times and in all places.'[7]

Jehovah is the LORD, the Almighty God. He can always be trusted and always relied upon. He met the needs of Gideon and Asa, and will meet ours. To emphasize this Scripture reveals God to us in names in compound with Jehovah.

Jehovah Jireh	the LORD will provide
Jehovah Rapha	the LORD who heals you
Jehovah Nissa	the LORD our banner
Jehovah Shalom	the LORD our peace
Jehovah Roi	the LORD our shepherd
Jehovah Tsidkenu	the LORD our righteousness
Jehovah Shammah	the LORD is present here

This is the almighty Lord who is our God. If we would but believe him and trust him, our fears and frustrations and failures would not be so frequent. If we really believed the LORD is all he claims to be, it would change our whole approach to church life. Of course we pay lip-service to the need for the presence of God, but our expectation is too dependent upon the man in the pulpit and not on the God upon the throne. We forget that all the time the Lord is present. He says, 'I am *Jehovah Shammah*

— I am in the midst of you. Look to me. Talk to me.' God is not a million miles away. The same Lord also says to us, 'I am *Jehovah Nissi* — your banner of victory. I will not allow my work to suffer. Your victory does not depend upon yourselves but upon me.'

All these things would be a tremendous encouragement to us if we really believed them. Everything we need as Christians we have in Jehovah. Our problem is expressed in Isaiah 43:22: 'Yet you have not called upon me, O Jacob, you have not wearied yourselves for me, O Israel.' Calling upon the Lord is not something casual but involves effort, sweat and tears. It means wearying ourselves. Often we do not do this because over the years we have lost hope and expectancy. We do not believe things can change. But the Lord says, 'I am doing a new thing' (Isa. 43:19). He promises to make a way in the desert and streams in the waste lands. We can see the spiritual desert of our nation, the moral wastelands of our towns and cities. We feel so helpless, but God says, 'You may not be able to do anything, but I can. You are weak, but I am the Lord almighty. Look to me. Trust me. Call upon me.'

All this must surely give us confidence in the Lord. There is no need for any Christian to be downhearted. It is true that there is a certain logic about unbelief. How can we hope to change the world? It sounds absurd and it is absurd. But the voice of Jehovah says, 'You cannot but I can.'

Two Old Testament examples

To encourage ourselves let us conclude by looking at two more Old Testament characters.

Abraham, in Genesis 22, was in serious trouble. He was being asked to sacrifice his son Isaac. This was an enormous test of his faith but he believed God. When Isaac asked where the lamb was for the burnt offering, Abraham answered, 'God himself will provide the lamb.' He had no direct promise to that effect, but he knew his God and trusted him. As you read the story you see that the Lord did provide the sacrifice and Abraham named the place *Jehovah-Jireh*, 'The Lord will provide'.

Jeremiah had a hard ministry. God's people were being plagued by false prophets and they preferred to listen to them rather than to God's true prophet, Jeremiah. Everything seemed lost. No one would believe the truth. Then God made a great promise:

'The days are coming,' declares the Lord,
  'when I will raise up to David a righteous Branch,
a King who will reign wisely
  and do what is just and right in the land'

(Jer. 23:5)

Who is this King going to be? He is *Jehovah Tsidkenu* — the Lord our righteousness. What hope and comfort this is! Jesus is our righteousness. We have no hope apart from this. All our righteousness is like a pile of filthy rags in God's sight and we are totally unacceptable to the Lord. But there is another righteousness for us, the righteousness of God, *Jehovah Tsidkenu*. Our hope is in the love and mercy and provision of God. It always is. If we look to ourselves and our problems, we shall despair. But once Jehovah is added to our thinking, all changes.

Let's give the final word to Tozer: 'Since I have been a Christian, I have lived to hear God say, "I am who I am. You can't, but I can. You aren't, but I am. You are not able, but I am able. You have no wisdom, but I am Jehovah and I have the wisdom." We approach him through Jesus Christ, his Son. Never forget that all the power of this great Jehovah with his awful and awesome glorious names is channelled through the person of his Son, Jesus Christ, to his people. Jesus dug a channel, so to speak, through to the mighty ocean that is Jehovah, so all the sweet waters, the healing waters, the soul-quenching waters that are God can flow down to the Lord's people if they would only believe.'[8]

Notes

1. C. H. Spurgeon, *Treasury of David,* Marshall, Morgan and Scott, 1957, vol. 2, p.448.
2. A. W. Pink, *The Life of David,* Baker Book House, 1985, vol. 2, p.118.
3. Edward Morgan, *John Elias, Life and Letters,* Banner of Truth, 1973, p.138.
4. D. M. Lloyd-Jones, *Revival,* Marshall Pickering, 1986, p.251.
5. A. W. Tozer, *Out of the Rut into Revival,* Hodder & Stoughton, 1993, p.152.
6. As above.
7. J. I .Packer, *God's Words,* IVP, 1981, p.47.
8. Tozer, *Out of the Rut into Revival,* p.161.